MW00529718

# The Smell of Rust

# The Smell of Rust

Haiku
by Margaret Chula

Cover Photograph
by John A. Hall

Katsura Press
2003

Publications by Margaret Chula

*Always Filling, Always Full*, 2001
*Grinding my ink* CD (with Ken Ulansey), 2000
*Shadow Lines* (with Rich Youmans), 1999
*This Moment*, 1995
*Grinding my ink*, 1993

The author would like to thank Claire Gallagher, Garry Gay, and Jerry Kilbride for reading the original manuscript and offering comments for the back cover; Marian Olson for writing an eloquent foreword; Caroline Enns for supplying the scans; and, as always, John for enriching the book with his photograph and my life with his presence.

Published by Katsura Press
P.O. Box 275
Lake Oswego, OR 97034

Library of Congress Control Number 2003092079
International Standard Book Number 0-9638551-2-3

Printed on recycled, acid-free paper

*For my mother*
*Adelia*

# Foreword

I discovered Margaret Chula's poetry when reading *Grinding my ink*, her first book of haiku. She appeared like a genie out of air and then she won the prestigious Haiku Society of America's Merit Book Award for it, a stunning coup among a bank of seasoned American haiku poets. And no wonder. The book was outstanding, "the harvest of a quiet eye," as William Wordsworth might have said. I didn't know her but, by the time I finished the book, she had me under her spell.

Who was this woman with a golden tongue?

A native of Northfield, Massachusetts, Chula spent the long hours of her youth exploring the eighty acres of her grandparents' farm. There she discovered the wonders of nature which fueled her adventurous soul. Her innate curiosity continued to flourish and as a young woman, she left the United States and began a journey that led her around the world. Japan captured her interest, in particular the old capital, Kyoto, where she settled for twelve years in a little wooden house with her husband and steeped herself in East Asian culture. During those years she learned the craft of haiku. William J. Higginson, translator and scholar of Japanese poetic forms, has remarked that Chula's work blends "acute perception with the grace and aesthetics of the [Japanese] tradition."

Was it luck or the poetic muse that gave Chula the title for *The Smell of Rust*? At once sensory and allusive, the image opens the imagination, just as a fine haiku will. The physical presence of rust suggests the temporal and with it the awareness of cycles, that every end is a beginning. John Hall's impressionistic color photograph on the cover augments these associations and reinforces the tone, establishing a subtle resonance with her poetry.

Throughout the text, Chula weaves rengay and haiku sequences with haiku and *senryu* to reflect life's dynamic flux, an important editorial decision since haiku arranged by season in haiku collections today have become a cliché. The poems in *The Smell of Rust* are as natural as lichen growing on solid surfaces, with a range of perceptions as varied as life itself, from the erotic "just a faint tinge / of pink on the goblet / put your mouth there" to the humorous "Halloween party / the plastic surgeon / comes as himself" to the philosophical "late into the night / we talk of revelations / moon through the pines" to the keenly beautiful "carrying moonlight / into the house / white peony." Poems such as these are not the exception in this collection of exceptional poems. The brushstrokes of her poetic lines unfold with the precision of a *sumi-e* master to reveal tiny parcels of subtle beauty— the mark of her haiku.

Margaret Chula has done it again: she has cast another bewitching spell in the latest book of poems. *The Smell of Rust* is magic.

Marian Olson
Santa Fe, New Mexico
February 2003

*The notes I handle no better than many pianists.*
*But the pauses between the notes—ah, that is*
*where the art resides.*

Artur Schnabel

*Tell all the Truth but tell it slant*
*Success in Circuit lies*
*Too bright for our infirm Delight*
*The Truth's superb surprise*

Emily Dickinson

carrying moonlight
into the house
white peony

sultry afternoon
in Grandma's junk mail
Frederick's of Hollywood




nourished by crude seeds
yet how beautifully
the song sparrow sings

silk sheets
  gardenia on the bed stand
  unfolds its petals




              abandoned koto
              the spider's spindly legs
              play a silent tune

mountain stream
    a raccoon bends
to lick the moon




somehow comforting
the call of the mourning dove
through rain

end of summer
the rust on my scissors
smells of marigolds

his unpacking
comes to a halt
—her old diary


through the rain
a riff of bird song
camellias half open


spring breeze
scented with wistaria
    my just-washed hair

cupping a firefly
I feel its light tremble
against my palm


pollen of a cattail
this brightness
just before sunset

long after they're gone
    I see the wild geese flying
across an empty sky




milkweed seeds
burst out of their pods
chirr of crickets

mosquitoes swarm—
the dinner conversation
sharpens

call from an old friend
first hummingbird
at the fuchsia


                    searching for what—
                    ant in the stone garden
                    climbing up, climbing down

mid-summer drought
      chickens
take a dirt bath


remembering those gone
thankful to be here—
pond of purple iris

listening
to the Zen master speak
        on and on and on

blade of summer grass
its sweetness
cuts my tongue

between red berries
and my ikebana shears
—swamp

# Hush

Rengay by Margaret Chula and *Cherie Hunter Day*

crescent moon
fingernail clippings
in a glass bowl

*bite marks darken the flesh*
*of an Anjou pear*

drawing customers
with those red lips, porcelain skin
store mannequin

*left behind*
*in the confessional*
*scent of her perfume*

hushed whispers at twilight
pierced by the whippoorwill's call

*cloudburst—*
*hailstones lodge in the folds*
*of a camellia*

winter morning
the red eye
of the towhee



burying my aunt
her prize-winning tulips
sprout in the wood shed

New Year's Day
my overalls stained
with last year's garden

late into the night
we talk of revelations
moon through the pines


summer solstice
skinny dipping in the river
jingle of bracelets


non-stop newscasts
I keep my ears tuned
to evening crickets

Early Girl tomatoes
turn from green to red
on the compost heap


twilight
the blur of hydrangeas
deepens

in the gardener's shed
an abundance
of left-handed gloves




flinging it into
the old growth forest
broken toothpick

Indian summer
the ground-fall pear
warm in my hand


                                rain-splattered fence
                                  a snail inches up
                                    to the spot of sun

missing you
the long-awaited fragrance
of paperwhites




branches wrapped in ice
a small gray moth, still
against my window

spring wind
    raked stones in the dry garden
flow without moving

nursing home
she rubs my lipstick kiss
into her cheeks




breaking my diet
with mocha fudge ice cream
—hole in the cone




Indian summer
the smell of rotting apples
on the wings of wasps

birdbath
a purple finch
scatters the sunset


after months of rain
the play of light and shadow
—gnats swarm

seeking truth
the deep pink center
of azaleas




this dreary morning—
winding a bright silk scarf
over my sweater

looking down from the pass
at the fear left behind
a forest of mist

all night the pain—
now, through a torn screen
chickadee's song


breaking up
she sprays his bedroom
with her perfume

they bloom
to please no one
    mountain cherries


Halloween party
the plastic surgeon
comes as himself

summer morning
the tiger lilies open
to the hummingbird



just a faint tinge
of pink on the goblet
put your mouth there

Tanabata
in the mailbox a letter
from an old lover

Tanabata is a Japanese festival celebrated on the seventh
day of the seventh month. On this day, Altair and Vega,
lovers separated by the Milky Way, are allowed to meet.

a month of rain
and not one
edible mushroom


bulldozerobins


morning frost
       stutter
of the rooster

fermented apples—
in a nearby pasture
horses nibble the air


Weight Watchers' potluck
a wide array
of Jell-O salads

impossible
to add to its beauty—yet
light on the peony




depth of winter
snow is white
limbs are black

this moment
is all—cracks
in the stone Buddha

# So Much For Nothing

cushion, incense, bowl
so much preparation
to do nothing


Buddha's birthday
I open a new
box of incense


meditation—
before striking the bell
I hear the bell


for a moment
nothingness—then
noticing it

imagining
myself as a Buddha
my limbs turn to bronze


sudden draft
the candle flickers
and drowns in itself


after meditation
I sit and meditate
smell of candle wax

gliding like a twig
he goes where the river goes...
to the other shore

for Bob Spiess


winter darkness
rain washes light
into the pine needles

reflecting
on the pond's reflections
dragonfly and I


summer camp
every day
a new best friend

crow
feasting on road kill
    road kill




up to their necks
in lawn daisies
the robin    the worm

Easter morning
the bread dough breathes and rises
under its damp cloth

sawing off the limb—
a column of ants marches
    to the tip


        while he brushes
        the strokes for "spring wind"
        the monk's eyebrows rise

the bruised scent
of rosemary on my hands
winter twilight


days lengthen
    the amaryllis topples
        under its own weight

trapeze artist
tattoo of a crane
on her shoulder

the way
koi pleat the water
my lips open

summer of love
the surfboard
still in its sheath

at dusk
call of a distant owl
snowflakes thicken




                    waking this morning
                    from troubled dreams—
                    fox prints on new snow

grasshoppers
zizz & jump    zizz & jump
        cat pounces




all around
the newly dug grave
mole holes

summer's end
spider webs cling to
all the dead flowers


                    chickens no longer
                    dash to the compost—
                    dregs of Chinese herbs

from the porch glider
the smell of jasmine
he turns off the light




my tears come
then the sound
spring rain

library book
on living simply
two weeks overdue


jogging on
the dog checks his messages
at every tree

autumn equinox
my smoke alarm
starts chirping


just before
he lights the firecracker
fireflies!

# Boston Public Garden

Rengay by Helen K. Davie and *Margaret Chula*


city park
the woman in a straw hat
walks from shade to shade

> *young lovers in the swan boat*
> *lick the same cone*

six ducklings
the mother duck dives
under their reflections

*making a wide arc*
*around the homeless—*
*pigeons and tourists*

> crossing the bridge
> your arm encircles my waist

*soap bubbles*
*hold the summer scene*
> *then burst*

harmony
a robin's egg
lands whole on a rock

first violets
a letter arrives
from you
      for Edith Shiffert

warmth of the tearoom
the colored leaves
turn into themselves

like an artist's seal
hoofprints of wild horses
claim the muddy road


                         encircling
                      Mount Rainier
                     a boa of clouds

morning fog
a gray heron
stitches sky to sea


marking her place
in the low-cal cookbook
chocolate bar wrapper

terrorist attack—
in the orchard
green apples


winter frost
the crow quick-steps
for his breakfast

dreaming of you
this morning molehills
erupt from the lawn

the scent of his wife
held in the widower's hand
magnolia petals




across from the graveyard
stork lawn ornament
"It's a boy!"

while I meditate
on nonattachment
a mosquito bites my leg

# Human Stones

outdoor sitting—
hard under my limbs
the ancient roots of trees

breathing in, breathing out
wind brings the scent of incense
and takes it away

meditation
dead leaves
in our sandals

cry of crickets
at the height of summer
   we shift positions

seated all in a row
silent human stones
for flies to land on

buzz of a fly
hum of a lawn mower
     stillness

meandering stream—
the shape of the pond
as it fills


fold it in thirds
our yoga teacher says
    the blanket, that is

soaking in the hot tub
   snail on the curtain
  taking the vapors




        gibbous moon
        a raccoon presses his face
        against our window

jet-lagged—
all night the mockingbird
tells me it's dawn


setting off the alarm
at airport security
nipple ring


old pond
a carp jumps
over the moon

lying on tatami
in a room full of fireflies
    the evening cool


how musty
the woolen clothes
white chrysanthemums

clearing the spider's web
off my face
I walk into fog




unrelenting beat
of a dragonfly's wings
light and shadow

from pink petunias
to the Budweiser sign
hummingbird

illegal parking
stuck behind my wiper blade
a withered oak leaf

today crickets
and the sun dim on my face
herbs gone to seed

drought
the click of squirrel's claws
on dry bark


war begins—
my husband and I
stop bickering

winter fog
  all my New Year's resolutions
    disappear


        hailstones
        the staccato song
        of wind chimes

my cousin
on life support
stubble on his chin


icicles melt—
I read the poems
of Robert Frost

# Searching for Emily

Emily Dickinson
Born December 10, 1830
Called Back May 15, 1886


I ask the U.P.S. man
Is this the cemetery where
Emily Dickinson is buried?
    "Don't know. We don't deliver
    too many packages there."


next to the site
where Emily is buried
Central Travel


Why am I wandering
in this stifling heat
searching for her grave
when I don't even
understand her poems?


scattered here and there
so many generations
of Dickinsons

nearly tripping over
a long-buried stone
with no name


searching
the bumble bee flits
from clover to clover


it's not the biggest
nor the tallest
Emily's gravestone


the only tombstone
covered with green moss
her green thumb


in the family plot
a dying hemlock—Emily
would have watered it


good luck stones
placed by tourists on top
of the family graves
    thirteen for Emily
    two for Lavinia

so much space
for such
a frail body


a single daisy
on her headstone
three petals torn off
        he loves her!


tiny grasshoppers
jump onto my poem, jump
onto her name


shadows of a lattice gate
reflected on her gravestone
her lacy white dress


writing a poem
I bury it in the crabgrass
at the base of her grave

reading the "personals"
a man at the next table
looks over and smiles


heat lightning—
my brother ignites firecrackers
with a blowtorch

lung tumor
she plants tulip bulbs
close to the surface

for years I tracked him
with birding binoculars
the boy next door


catalpa blossoms—
falling in love with
the girl I once was

night of the new moon
I crave nothing, no one
frogs croaking, croaking


depth of winter
rubbing more face cream
into my crow's-feet

in the flutter
of a hummingbird's wing
    last night's dream




now I understand
the jewel in the lotus
dewdrops

wind at twilight
the scent of apple blossoms
apple blossoms

## Publications

*Kyoto Journal, Heron's Nest, Modern Haiku, Frogpond, Tundra, Woodnotes, LYNX, Bottle Rockets, Albatross, Geppo, Mainichi Shimbun, The Best of the Electronic Poetry Network* (Shreveport Regional Arts Council), *Symbiotic Poetry, AHA Online Anthology*

## Anthologies

*Global Haiku, Twenty Haiku Poets from Around the World,* Ironwood Press, England
*Stone Bench in the Empty Park*, Orchard Books, NY
*Young Leaves: An Old Way of Seeing New,* Yuki Teikei Society
*Haikukai* (Japan), Introducing Northwest Regional Poets
*Haiku Anthology*, edited by Cor van den Heuvel, W.W. Norton
*Crinkled Sunshine*, Haiku Society of America Members' Anthology
*Intersections*, HSA Members' Anthology
*Shades of Green*, Haiku North America Conference, Press Here
*Peace Poetry Across the Pacific*, University of Hawaii Press
*Dreams Wander*, HSA Members' Anthology
*Haiku Moment: An Anthology of North American Haiku*, Charles E. Tuttle Co.
HSA Northwest Regional Anthologies: *Haiku in 3-D; On Crimson Wings* (Japanese Centennial Anthology); *to find the words; Cherry Blossom Rain; Unbroken Curve; Sunlight Through Rain; Sudden Shower; Echoes Across the Cascades*

## Awards

| | |
|---|---|
| "Easter morning" | First Prize, Yuki Teikei Contest |
| "through the rain" | Editor's Choice, Heron's Nest |
| "blowing soap bubbles" | Second Prize, Yuki Teikei Contest |
| "mosquitoes swarm" | Courage Award, Ocha New Haiku Contest |
| "cupping a firefly" | Inspiration Award, First International Haiku Festa, Japan |
| "spring wind" | Second Prize Mainichi Haiku Contest |
| "late into the night" | Honorable Mention, HSA Harold Henderson Contest |
| "long after they're gone" | Winner, Kumamoto Contest |

**Margaret Chula** lived in Kyoto for twelve years, where she taught creative writing at Kyoto Seika University and Doshisha Women's College. While in Japan, she studied *hanga* (woodblock printing) and ikebana, receiving a teacher's license from the Sogetsu school. Her award-winning books include *Grinding my ink*, *This Moment*, *Shadow Lines* (linked *haibun* with Rich Youmans) and *Always Filling, Always Full*. Her haiku have been anthologized in *Global Haiku: Twenty Haiku Poets from Around the World*; *The Haiku Anthology*; and *Haiku Moment: An Anthology of North American Haiku*.

Active in the international haiku community, Ms. Chula has been a featured speaker for the Haiku Society of America, the Yuki Teikei Society, and Haiku North America. She was on the organizing committee for the Haiku North America conference held in Portland, Oregon in 1997 and selected as a delegate to the Haiku International Association conference in Tokyo.

Now living in Portland, Oregon, she continues to teach, giving lectures and workshops at universities, Zen centers, and in the Artists in the Schools Program. As a Board Member of the Asian Arts Council at the Portland Art Museum, she is responsible for planning Japanese-related events for the community. Grants from Oregon Literary Arts and the Regional Arts and Culture Council have supported collaborations with artists, musicians, photographers, and dancers.

# Colophon

Design and layout by John A. Hall
Set in Adobe Garamond
Printed on Cougar Natural Opaque stock
by Lithtex Printing Solutions, Hillsboro, Oregon
Author's photo by John A. Hall